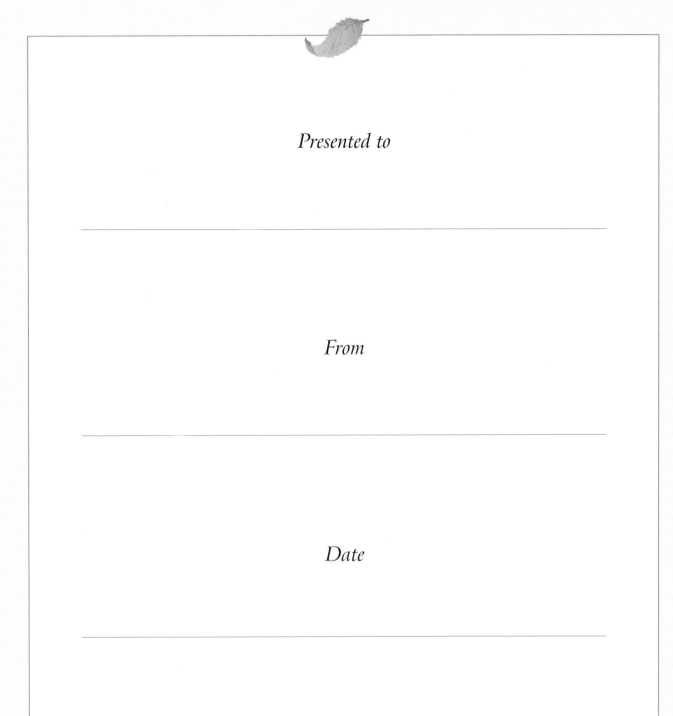

Presented to

_____

From

_____

Date

_____

CROSSWAY BOOKS BY JONI EARECKSON TADA

I'll Be With You Always
The Incredible Discovery of Lindsey Renee
You've Got a Friend
On the Wings of the West Wind

Darcy and Friends Series with Steve Jensen
  The Amazing Secret
  The Meanest Teacher
  The Mission Adventure
  The Unforgettable Summer

**Great Hymns of the Faith Series
with John MacArthur and Robert and Bobbie Wolgemuth**
  O Worship the King
  O Come All Ye Faithful
  What Wondrous Love Is This

Tell Me Series with Steve Jensen
  Tell Me the Truth
  Tell Me the Promises

**The Toy Shoppe on Periwinkle Lane Series
with Melody Carlson**
  Forever Friends

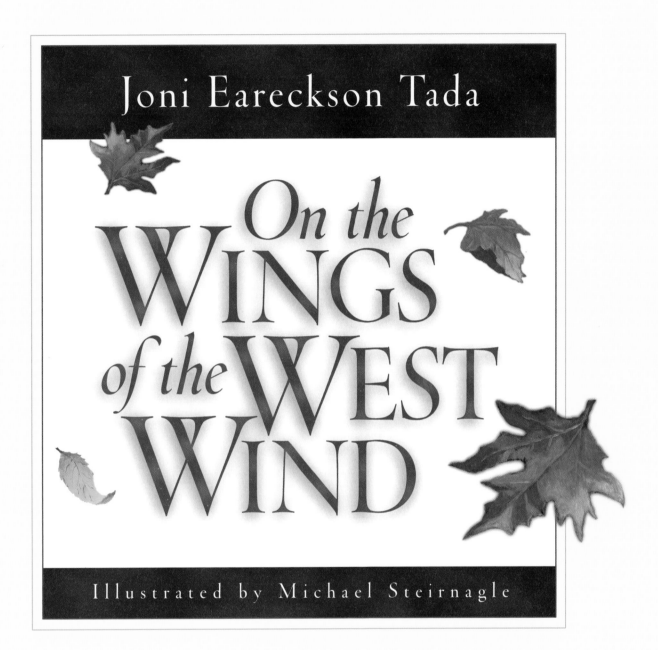

Joni Eareckson Tada

On the Wings of the West Wind

Illustrated by Michael Steirnagle

CROSSWAY BOOKS

A DIVISION OF GOOD NEWS PUBLISHERS, WHEATON, ILLINOIS

PUBLISHER'S ACKNOWLEDGMENT

The publisher wishes to acknowledge that the text for *On the Wings of the West Wind* appeared originally as "Chains That Bind Can Be Broken" in *Tell Me the Truth*, copyright ©1997, written by Joni Eareckson Tada and Steve Jensen and illustrated by Ron DiCianni. Special thanks to Ron DiCianni for the idea and vision behind the creation of the series. More stories in the Tell Me series—*Tell Me the Story*, *Tell Me the Secrets*, *Tell Me the Promises*, and *Tell Me Why*, all published by Crossway Books—are available at your local bookstore.

On the Wings of the West Wind

Text copyright © 1997 by Joni Eareckson Tada

Illustrations copyright © 2002 by Michael Steirnagle

Published by Crossway Books
a division of Good News Publishers
1300 Crescent Street, Wheaton, Illinois 60187

Book design by Cindy Kiple

First printing 2002

Printed in the United States of America

ISBN 1-58134-372-8

LIBRARY OF CONGRESS CATALOGING-IN-PUBLICATION DATE

Tada, Joni Eareckson.
    On the wings of the west wind / text by Joni Eareckson Tada;
illustrated by Michael Steirnagle.
      p. cm.
    Summary: Marcus has been a slave his entire life, dreaming of freedom,
until the day a boy arrives on the wings of the west wind with a message from
another master, the King.
    ISBN 1-58134-372-8 (alk. paper)
    [1. Slaves--Fiction. 2. Freedom--Fiction. 3.Christian life--Fiction.]
I. Steirnagle, Michael, ill. II. Title.
    PZ7.T116 On 2002
    [Fic]--dc21

                                                                                                2001006503

For my friends—

Matthew, Stephen, and Daniel Fenlason

Marcus couldn't remember a time when his chains did not tear into his ankles and wrists, rubbing the skin raw. The chains reminded him of his shame, for he was a slave of the wicked master of the field in which he worked. Marcus had never known freedom. He wasn't even sure what it was. But every once in a while, especially when the west wind blew in, he caught the scent of something fresh and good. He'd breathe deeply and wonder what it would be like to live without chains. That, he decided, would be freedom indeed.

Marcus loved the smell of freedom. It was all he had. For not only was he bound by chains, but he could barely see. More than that, he could hardly hear. It was the same for the other slaves he worked with in the field. What a sad and terrible life they lived!

Suddenly Marcus felt the sting of a whip across his back. It was his master. He felt a shove and a kick. With a groan, he lifted his chains and went back to moving rocks and dirt. Never was there a more tiring job. Marcus and the other slaves worked with heads low. They were not allowed ever to raise their heads for fear that they might catch the scent of freedom when the west wind blew. Their job also made no sense—all they did was move rocks and shovel dirt from one place to another.

One day when his chains seemed especially heavy, Marcus felt an urgent tug in his heart. The west wind was blowing in. He dared to raise his head, drawing in a deep breath of sweet, fresh air. *Yes*, he thought, *it is the beautiful scent of freedom.* Today, however, freedom felt especially close, much nearer than ever before—so near that it seemed as though the figure of freedom was standing next to him. He turned in its direction. Rubbing and blinking his eyes, he thought he saw—yes, he could see!—the blurry form of a boy with no chains on, smiling with eyes sparkling.

"I have come on the wings of the west wind, carrying a message from my master, the King. He has sent me to give you his good news. The news is: 'You shall know the truth, and the truth will set you free.' Do you wish to be free?" the boy asked with a bigger smile. "Do you wish to leave this terrible place and join me in my master's field?"

"D-do I wish to be free?" Marcus stammered. He stared until the figure of the boy became sharp and clear. "Of course!" Marcus exclaimed. Not only was he now able to see, but he could actually hear the words sent by the King.

"Then you must leave your chains behind," the boy said.

Marcus looked down. "But I can't," he cried. "I can't break these chains!"

The boy spoke again. "Know the truth. It will set you free. Come and follow me."

Marcus's heart sank, but he found enough courage to reach for the boy's hand. When he did, to his surprise, his chains unlocked and fell to the ground. With that, the boy grasped Marcus's hand and led him out of the rocky, dirty field, through a gate in a stone wall, and into a green pasture with trees, flowers, and a beautiful brook that flowed from tall mountains in the distance. People were happily working in the fields where corn and wheat were growing. Things grew here! What's more, the pasture smelled heavenly—just like freedom *should* smell.

Marcus thanked the boy and then turned around to see the happy face of his new master, the King.

"Come into my field prepared for you," the King said. "I am your master, and you will no longer be called a slave, but my friend."

Marcus could hardly believe it! He had been rescued. Saved. Best of all, his chains were gone. He rubbed his ankles and wrists in delight. "No more chains—I'm free!" he shouted happily. "I no longer serve that wicked ruler in the old field."

The master of the beautiful pasture smiled and reminded him of one more important fact: "And don't forget, you now have eyes to see the truth and ears to hear my word. Never forget that."

Marcus was glad to see there were others in the pasture. These were free people who had been rescued from the awful field, too. Even the boy who led Marcus out had once been a slave. And like the boy, many free people asked their kind master if they could go back to the old field when the west wind blew so that they could rescue their fellow slaves—just as the boy had rescued Marcus. The kind master always gave them his blessing but warned them to be careful to obey his voice and never to forget the way back through the gate in the stone wall.

One day, after many months of exploring the beautiful pasture, Marcus wandered along the stone wall until he came to the gate through which he had been led into freedom. He became curious. He wondered what was happening on the other side. The kind master of the pasture was nowhere in sight. The west wind was not blowing. His friends had gone on a journey to the great mountains. Marcus decided to peek through the gate.

When he did, he heard a frightening sound. "What are you doing on that side of the stone wall?" a voice growled.

Marcus knew at once that this was the voice of his old master—the wicked ruler of the field of dirt and rocks. Marcus shivered with fear. Always before he had been deaf and blind to the ways of the old master. Back then he had only obeyed the whip and the kicks and shoves like an animal. But now he realized his old master had a voice—a very powerful and forceful voice.

"Get back in here where you belong!" the wicked ruler snarled. "You don't belong over in that pasture with those people who are free. You belong here. This is where you're supposed to be!"

Marcus's mouth went dry, and his breath came in short gasps. He wanted to turn around, but he froze.

The old master hollered again, "I said, get in here. Now!"

At the word "Now!" Marcus jumped. He stumbled into the field of dirt and rocks and saw for the first time the shape of his evil master—a frightening, huge, strong, dark shape. The old master puffed out his chest. Marcus stooped low, just like he used to with his head down. He looked around and saw the poor slaves, none of them able to see or hear him.

"I know what you're thinking," the wicked ruler sneered as he came up to Marcus. "You think you're just going to visit here."

Marcus was amazed—that was exactly what he was thinking!

His old master laughed. "You can forget that idea right now. Here," he said as he threw a set of chains on the ground, "put these on!"

Marcus looked at the chains, remembering how they felt against his skin. Nothing made him see more clearly the horror of life in this terrible place than those dreadful, heavy chains.

The crack of a whip startled him. The wicked master yelled more loudly, "I demand that you put these chains on! Right away!" Marcus's knees knocked, and his legs trembled. He felt helpless. He felt he had to obey. He had no other choice. Sadly, he bent over and started putting the cuffs around his wrists.

At that instant a gentle wind touched his face. It was the west wind, carrying the words of the King. The words were faint, much fainter than if he heard them in the beautiful pasture, but Marcus could hear them just the same: "The truth will set you free." Yes, yes, it was the sound of the voice of his wonderful friend—his King, his new master!

The wicked ruler snapped, "That fool has no say over what you do in *this* field. Put on those chains. You're mine!"

Marcus was torn. Why didn't the King come and rescue him? His heart breaking, Marcus cried toward the gate in the stone wall, "Please, come help me. Please, save me!"

But no one came. The west wind blew harder, and the wicked master roared even more loudly.

Again the words of the King lifted on the breeze: "You shall know the truth, and the truth shall set you free."

"Don't listen to those lies!" the angry man before him warned, holding his whip high, as if to strike.

Just then a light dawned in Marcus's mind. The wicked master had not struck out with his whip. He had not kicked or shoved him like he used to. *In fact,* Marcus realized, *he has not laid a hand on me at all.*

He straightened up and raised his head high. His fear left. Now he understood the power behind the words of his friend, the King. Marcus really was free—it didn't look like it, it didn't feel like it, but that didn't change the truth that he *was free*. The words of the King were all he needed. He finally realized that this angry, red-faced ruler had no power over him at all.

Marcus looked him straight in the eye. "You are the one who is a liar," Marcus said to him, "and you have no right to boss me around. I belong to the King, and my place is in his green pastures."

To Marcus's amazement, the wicked master backed off, like a snake crawling away, like a coward slinking away from the face of courage.

Marcus turned around and walked directly toward the gate in the stone wall, into the good master's open arms. Marcus had almost forgotten how sweet and delightful the King's pasture was. He saw his friends. He saw the boy who had first led him to safety. He breathed in deeply the delightful smell of freedom.

"You must never think that you *have* to obey that old snake," the kind King said softly. Then he sighed with a smile, as if holding back something sad. "But the stone wall cannot keep out the sound of his voice. The west wind, on some days, will be still. Your friends will not always be near you, and even I," the King said warmly, "will not always seem to be near."

Marcus looked deeply into the eyes of his true master and nodded, understanding that these words would help him live the rest of his life in freedom.

The King continued, "Believe me when I say that although you can never change back into a slave again, you *do* have the choice to act like one, to live like one. The chains have no power over you that you do not give them. The power is in what you choose to believe." Tears filled Marcus's eyes—not tears of sadness, but of joy.

"Should you ever be bullied by that wicked master again," the King said, "keep this." He placed a piece of paper in Marcus's hands.

Marcus slowly unfolded it and read the most powerful and important words of all: "I am the way, the truth, and the life." Marcus looked up into the face of the King.

He realized that if he would remember this truth, he would always be free.

I am the Way
the Truth
and the
Life